This book belongs to:

_____

_____

The Farm

The Farm

ALAIN GRÉE

Button BOOKS

Publisher: Jonathan Bailey. Production Manager: Jim Bulley. Senior Project Editors: Sara Harper, Wendy McAngus. Managing Art Editor: Gilda Pacitti. Color origination: GMC Reprographics. Printed and bound in China.

Where does food come from?

It is breakfast time and we are eating toast and cereal. We put butter on the toast and milk on the cereal.

Max

Mary

"There isn't much milk left," says Mary. "Where can we buy some more?"

Dad buys our milk from the store, but how did it get there? Where does all the milk come from?

The Sunny Store

Open

Farm-fresh milk

7

Max explains that milk comes from cows on a farm.

farm

cow

milk

cereal

vegetables

meat

eggs

fruit

bread

Many of the things we eat and drink, and even things we wear, come from the farm.

butter

yarn

A letter has arrived from Aunt Helen. She has invited
us to visit her farm in the country. Let's go!

At the farm

Aunt Helen's farm is very busy. "There's lots of work," she says. "Would you like to help me and Uncle Henry?"

Aunt Helen

Uncle Henry

11

Let's explore the farm.
There is so much to see!

12

tractor

A tractor is a great way to get around the muddy farm.

Crops

The tractor is used to plant crops in the fields. Crops are plants that we can eat, such as vegetables or wheat.

The tractor pulls machinery that digs the field...

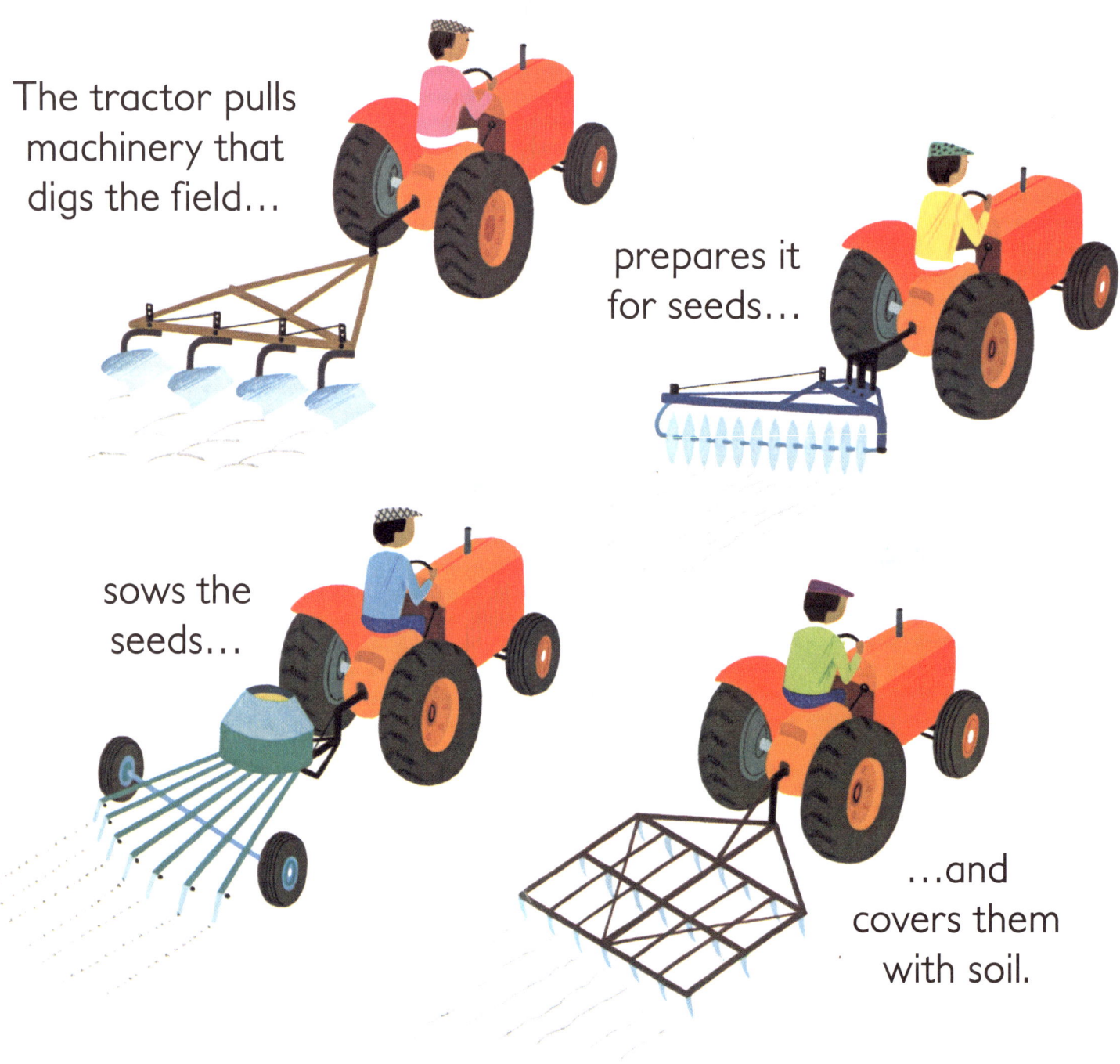

prepares it for seeds...

sows the seeds...

...and covers them with soil.

seeds

wheat

Today, we are planting seeds that will grow into wheat.
A scarecrow will stop the birds from eating the seeds.

scarecrow

When the wheat has grown tall and ripe, the farmer collects it with a big machine called a combine harvester.

16

The combine harvester collects the wheat
and separates the grain from it all at
once. The grain will be made into flour.

combine harvester

wheat

grain

17

Once the wheat has been harvested, the farmer plows the field, so it can be planted with seeds again.

plow

In the distance, on top of a hill, there is a strange building like a tower. Uncle Henry explains that it is a windmill.

windmill

sail

In the old days, grain was taken to a windmill to be ground into flour. The windmill's sails were turned by wind power.

Today, flour is mostly made by big electric machines. No need for wind!

The story of bread

A farmer sows the wheat seeds in the fields.
When it is ripe, the wheat is harvested.

The grain is taken from the wheat and ground into flour.
Bakers use the flour to make loaves of bread.

The freshly baked bread is delivered to stores in a truck.
We can buy the bread at our local bakery or store.

As well as bread, flour is needed to make:

pizza

pasta

pie

cookies

cake

Fruit

Now we are helping pick apples. They grow on apple trees. Cherries, plums, and pears grow on trees, too.

cherries

pear

plums

Strawberries, melons, and raspberries also grow at the farm on smaller plants.

strawberry

melon

raspberry

apples

The fruit will be taken to markets
and stores where people can buy it.

Vegetables

Many kinds of vegetables grow on the farm.

vegetable oil

soup

frozen vegetables

canned beans

canned peas

fries

Vegetables are often sold in the stores as they are, but some are canned or frozen so they last longer. Some are made into other foods, such as soup, vegetable oil, or fries.

To grow potatoes, we plant
a potato in the ground.
Leaves and roots will grow
from it, then new potatoes
will grow from the roots.

The potatoes need rain and
sunshine to make them grow.

carrots

cabbage

apple

leeks

Do you know
which of these foods
grow in the ground
and which grow
on a tree?

turnip

cherries

potato

pear

plums

29

Not all crops grown on the farm are for people to eat.
The farmer also grows food for the many animals that
live there, and makes straw to keep them warm in winter.

Straw comes from the stems of crops that are dried in the sun. These farmers are making a barn cozy and warm for the animals that live in it. The straw is their bedding.

Milk

The cows come to this barn
every day to be milked.
We are going to help
Aunt Helen milk the cows.

milk can

bucket

cow

In the old days, the cows were milked by hand, but it's much quicker today with a milking machine.

milking machine

truck

When all the milk is ready, it is taken away by truck to the dairy.

Dairy products

At the dairy, the milk goes into bottles and cartons, ready to sell in the stores.

milk

At the dairy, some of the cows' milk is turned into delicious foods such as cheese, butter, and even ice cream!

bread

soup

butter

roast chicken

fruit juice

Can you spot which of these foods are made from milk?

yogurt

cream

cake

ice cream

Sheep

Next, we are going to visit the sheep.
Sheep like to be high up on the hills,
where they eat the long, green grass.

Sheep grow thick, woolly coats that keep them warm in cold weather.

In spring, when it is too hot for a woolly coat, the farmer cuts the wool—it's like a haircut for sheep! The wool can then be made into clothes that keep us cozy in winter.

yarn

sheep

clothes

rooster

hen

turkey

chicks

Birds and eggs

Back in the farmyard, we help feed the birds.
There are chickens and turkeys.

Uncle Henry tells us that a female chicken is
called a hen and a male chicken is a rooster.
Their babies are called chicks.

egg

We are going to collect the
hens' eggs. Some eggs are
for us to eat, and others
will hatch into little chicks.

Where does meat come from?

pigs

Now let's go feed the pigs.

Aunt Helen explains that pigs give us meat, such as ham and pork.

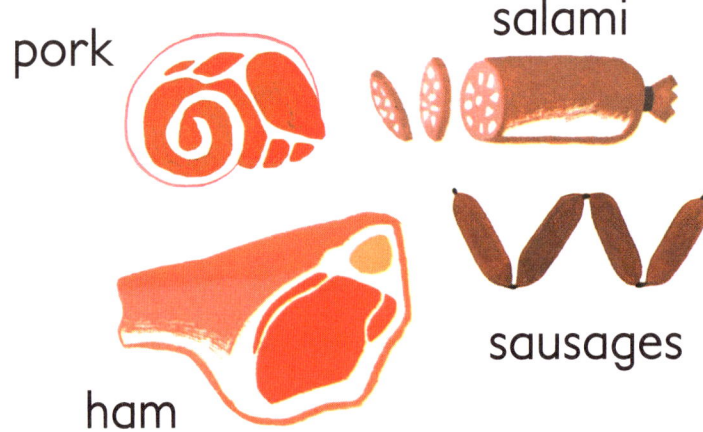

pork

salami

ham

sausages

40

peas

turkey

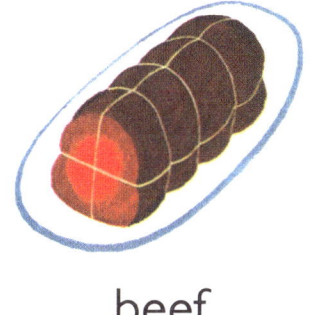
beef

milk

Other farm animals
give us meat, too.
Which of these foods
are types of meat?

cheese

chicken

eggs

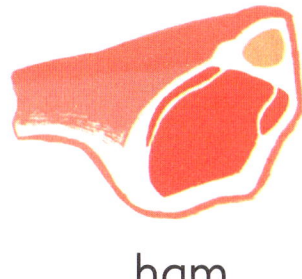
ham

On Aunt Helen's farm, we have met the animals and seen where our food comes from. It's time to go home. We feed the animals one last time and say goodbye.

When we arrive home from the farm, Mom and Dad have a surprise gift for us. What could it be?

It is a toy farm! There is even a tiny scarecrow.
Now we can play with the animals whenever we like.

Where does it come from?

ham

yogurt

eggs

bread

yarn

cheese

roast chicken

apple

pasta

Can you match the farm products above to what they come from on the opposite page?

wheat

apple tree

cow

pig

hen

sheep

ALAIN GRÉE

For more on Button Books, contact:

GMC Publications Ltd
Castle Place, 166 High Street, Lewes, East Sussex, BN7 1XU
United Kingdom
Tel +44 (0)1273 488005
www.buttonbooks.co.uk